Making a New Nation

A CHANGING NATION

Immigration and Industrialization
from the Civil War to World War I

Michael Burgan

HEINEMANN LIBRARY
CHICAGO, ILLINOIS

Designed by Philippa Baile and Kim Miracle
Maps by Jeff Edwards
Printed and bound in China by WKT Company Limited

11 10 09 08 07
10 9 8 7 6 5 4 3 2 1

Library of Congress Cataloging-in-Publication Data
Burgan, Michael.
  A changing nation / Michael Burgan.
    p. cm. -- (Making a new nation)
  Includes bibliographical references and index.
  ISBN 1-4034-7830-9 (library binding-hardcover) -- ISBN 1-4034-7837-6 (pbk.)
  1. United States--History--Juvenile literature.
  2. United States--Territorial expansion--History--Juvenile literature.
  3. United States--Emigration and immigration--History--Juvenile literature.
I. Title. II. Series.
  E178.5.B87 2006
  973--dc22
                          2006003251
Acknowledgments
The author and publisher are grateful to the following for permission to reproduce copyright material: AKG-Images p. **22**; Alamy Images p. **37** (Andre Jenny); Alamy Images/North Wind.Picture Archive p. **17**; Alamy Images/Popperfoto p. **40**; Corbis pp. **14** (S. D. Butcher), **15** (Andrew Joseph Russel), **20** (Lewis Hine), **23** (Russell Lee), **7**, **21**, **29**, **31**, **33**; Corbis/Bettmann pp. **5**, **8**, **10**, **24**, **34**, **35**; Getty Images/Hulton Archive pp. **18**, **38**; Getty Images/Kean Collection p. **26**; Getty Images/MPI p. **27**; Getty Images/Museum of the City of New York p. **16**; Getty Images/ Stock Montage p. **12**; Mary Evans Picture Library pp. **41**, **42**; Topfoto pp. **9** (Roger-Viollet), **19**, **39**; Topham Picturepoint p. **32**.

Cover photograph reproduced with the permission of The Granger Collection, New York.

The publishers would like to thank Kathryn Burns-Howard for her assistance in the preparation of this book.

Every effort has been made to contact copyright holders of any material reproduced in this book. Any omissions will be rectified in subsequent printings if notice is given to the publisher.

CONTENTS

Some words are shown in bold, **like this**. You can find out what they mean by looking in the glossary.

GROWTH AND GOLD

The United States won **independence** from Great Britain in 1783. At the time, the country's western **border** ended at the Mississippi River. In 1803 the United States bought a huge region west of the river called Louisiana. The Louisiana Purchase doubled the country's size.

HEADING WEST

Starting in the 1820s, some U.S. **settlers** went to Texas. At the time, Texas was part of Mexico. U.S. settlers helped Texas win its independence from Mexico in 1836. Then, in 1845, Texas became part of the United States.

Americans also moved into the Oregon Country. This region was west of the Rocky Mountains and north of California. The first Americans reached the area in the 1830s. Hundreds of thousands of people moved to this area in the decades after this. Many took a route across the United States called the Oregon Trail.

The settlers headed west for different reasons. Some wanted farmland, while others hoped to start businesses. Some Americans felt it was their duty to take control of the land and spread **democracy**. They called this manifest destiny.

Starting with the Louisiana Purchase, the borders of the United States expanded westward during the 1800s.

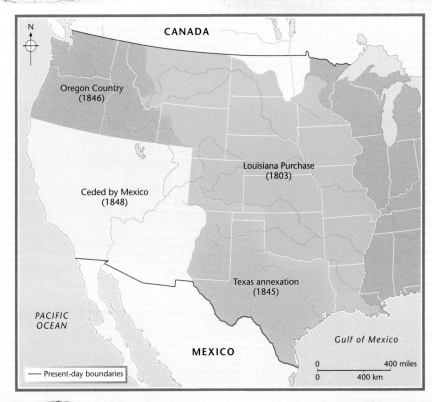

A WAR FOR LAND

In 1845 the United States and Mexico disagreed over the border between the two countries. President James K. Polk believed in manifest destiny. He wanted to take land from Mexico. Polk used the border dispute as an excuse to start a war. The Mexican War began in April 1846 and lasted two years. The United States won, and Mexico sold California and New Mexico to the United States. Americans now had new **territory** to settle in the West.

The Mormons

Unlike most settlers of the 1840s, the Mormons moved for religious reasons. Mormon beliefs angered some Americans. The Mormons decided to head west to find greater freedom. Brigham Young led a group of Mormons to Utah in 1847. Utah was still part of Mexico at the time. It became U.S. territory after the Mexican War.

The Battle of Palo Alto in May 1846 was the start of the Mexican War.

THE GOLD RUSH

Some Americans settled in California before it became U.S. territory. Even more came after gold was discovered there in 1848. News of the gold spread to other countries, including China. Thousands of Americans headed west to California. **Immigrants** soon joined them. Miners hoping to find great wealth created the California Gold Rush of 1849. In the decades to come, miners moved to other parts of the West. Gold, silver, and other minerals were discovered in places such as Nevada and Colorado.

The thirst for gold

A U.S. Army officer described what he saw at the start of the Gold Rush: "People, before engaged in [farming] and guarding their small herds of cattle and horses, have all gone to the mines....Laborers of every trade have left their workbenches, and tradesmen their shops. Sailors desert their ships as fast as they arrive on the coast."

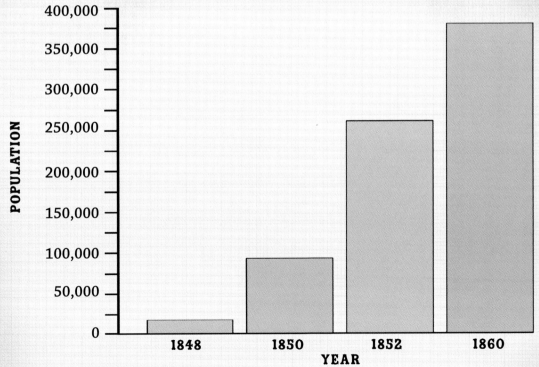

GROWTH IN NON-NATIVE AMERICAN POPULATION IN CALIFORNIA DUE TO THE GOLD RUSH

California became a state in 1850, following fast growth in its population due to the Gold Rush.

PROBLEMS FOR A GROWING NATION

Soon after the Gold Rush, the borders of the United States were in place. Americans had settled much of the country. Now, they prepared to develop the nation's valuable **natural resources**. These efforts would lead to the rise of new businesses and new cities. At the start of the 1800s, most Americans farmed to make a living. One hundred years later, millions worked in factories and stores instead.

The United States faced many challenges at this time. The country was divided over **slavery**. Native Americans wanted to keep their lands. The rise of industry created wealth for some, but many people faced harsh working conditions in factories and harsh living conditions at home. Millions of these workers were poor immigrants. Through the 1800s and into the 1900s, Americans debated how to deal with these issues.

San Francisco, shown here in 1855, had a population of 812 in 1848. By the end of the next year, it was 100,000.

THE SLAVERY PROBLEM

Adding California and New Mexico to the United States sparked a debate over slavery. At the time, slavery was legal in the South, but not in the North. Most southerners believed slavery should be allowed in new states and territories. Southern slave owners wanted the legal right to bring their slaves wherever they settled. Many northerners, however, opposed this. Free workers did not want to compete with slaves for jobs. Other Americans hated slavery on **moral** grounds. They were **abolitionists**. They wanted to abolish, or end, slavery everywhere in the United States.

An 1820 law called the Missouri **Compromise** had limited slavery in the states and territories carved out of the Louisiana Purchase. Except in Missouri, slavery was not allowed north of the 36° 30' **latitude**. Some southerners now wanted to extend that line through the new lands in the West. By extending the line, slavery would be allowed in some parts of California and New Mexico.

*The Compromise of 1850 also included the **Fugitive** Slave Law. This gave slave owners greater power to track down slaves who fled to free states.*

THE COMPROMISE OF 1850

Through 1849 the debate about slavery grew bitter. Some northern abolitionists thought the United States should split into two countries. One would allow slavery and one would not. Most lawmakers opposed this idea. They wanted to keep the country whole. Lawmakers came up with the Compromise of 1850. In 1850 California entered the country as a free state. New Mexico was divided into two territories: New Mexico and Utah. Residents there were given "popular sovereignty," which meant that they would choose whether or not to allow slavery.

Harriet Beecher Stowe

Harriet Beecher Stowe was an abolitionist. The Compromise of 1850 convinced her to speak out against slavery. In 1852 she published *Uncle Tom's Cabin*. The book looked at the horrors of slave life. The book angered southerners, but *Uncle Tom's Cabin* became popular around the world.

Slave owners sometimes whipped slaves who disobeyed.

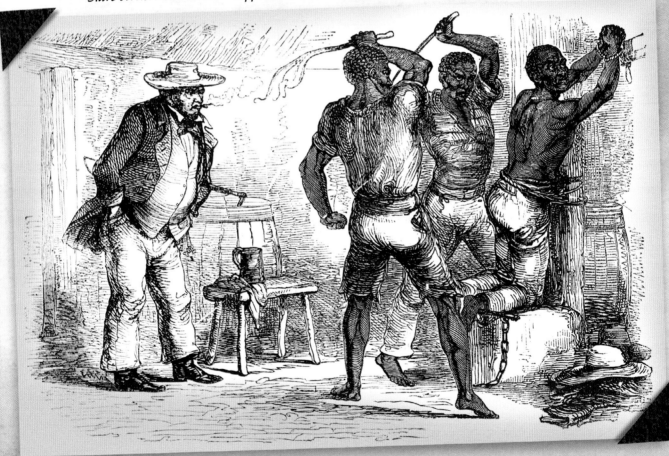

"BLEEDING KANSAS"

In 1854 the country once again debated slavery. **Congress** passed the Kansas-Nebraska Act. This law created two new territories in the northern part of the Louisiana Purchase and gave the settlers popular sovereignty. In doing so, the law overturned the old limit against extending slavery north of the 36° 30' latitude.

Most people did not expect slavery to be an issue in Nebraska. It bordered northern states that did not allow slavery. However, Kansas was next to the slave state of Missouri. Some Missouri slave owners had already moved into Kansas. Abolitionists opposed making slavery legal in Kansas. Both pro- and anti-slave settlers rushed to Kansas. Each side hoped to take control of the territory's government. Fighting between the two sides gave the area a new nickname: "Bleeding Kansas." After this struggle, Kansas became a free state when it entered the Union in January 1861.

In 1857 Missouri slave Dred Scott lost a legal battle to win his freedom, which made many abolitionists angry.

A DIVIDED NATION

In 1860 the Republican **Party** chose Abraham Lincoln to run for U.S. president. Lincoln and the Republicans opposed popular sovereignty. In a four-man race, Lincoln took enough northern states to win the election.

Lincoln believed that slavery was wrong, but he promised to continue to allow it where it already existed. Many southerners feared that Lincoln would not keep his promise. In South Carolina, lawmakers voted to **secede** from the Union. Ten other slave states eventually followed South Carolina. In 1861 they created the Confederate States of America. President Lincoln opposed this secession and would fight to keep the Union whole.

Lincoln on secession

"It was with the deepest regret that [I] found the duty of [using] the war-power, in defense of the government, forced upon [me]....And having thus chosen our course... let us renew our trust in God, and go forward without fear."

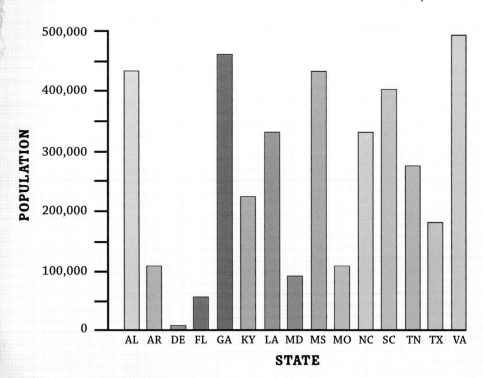

SLAVE POPULATION IN THE U.S., 1860

Of the states in the chart, Delaware, Missouri, Maryland, and Kentucky remained in the Union.

THE CIVIL WAR

The Civil War between the North and South began on April 12, 1861, at Fort Sumter, South Carolina. Lincoln soon called for 75,000 soldiers to help keep the Union whole. Southerners, meanwhile, eagerly volunteered to fight the North. They wanted to defend their states' rights, as spelled out in the U.S. **Constitution**.

The North had a larger army. Its factories could produce more weapons and supplies. It had more railroads. The South, however, had many skilled generals. They and their army were ready to protect their homeland against invading northern forces. Major fighting took place in almost every southern state. In some cases, members of the same family fought on opposing sides. Soldiers sometimes had to steal food from **civilians**, rather than eat the "bad beef and spoilt bread" the army gave them. Disease was common in the camps, and wounded soldiers usually did not receive good medical care.

In July 1863, the Battle of Gettysburg took place in Pennsylvania.

WINNING THE WAR

The Civil War dragged on for four years. By the war's end, the two sides had more than one million **casualties**. The North, with its greater wealth, finally won. Its victory kept the Union whole. Days after the war ended in April 1865, President Lincoln was shot and killed. Vice President Andrew Johnson then became president. He faced the difficult task of Reconstruction. The country had to rebuild after the damaging war.

Freeing the slaves

At first, Lincoln did not fight the Civil War to end slavery, but by 1863 he thought the North could not win if he did not abolish (end) it across the country. Abolishing slavery would win support from powerful foreign countries that opposed slavery. The North would also be able to recruit free blacks as soldiers. Lincoln first freed most slaves living in the South. Then, in 1865, the 13th **Amendment** to the Constitution ended slavery everywhere.

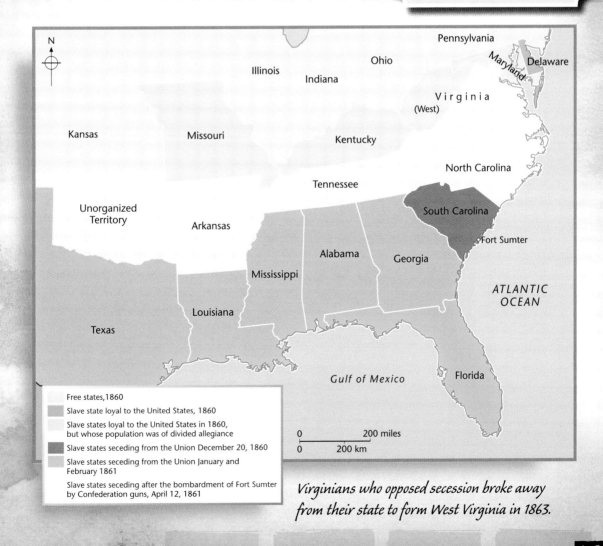

Free states, 1860

Slave state loyal to the United States, 1860

Slave states loyal to the United States in 1860, but whose population was of divided allegiance

Slave states seceding from the Union December 20, 1860

Slave states seceding from the Union January and February 1861

Slave states seceding after the bombardment of Fort Sumter by Confederation guns, April 12, 1861

Virginians who opposed secession broke away from their state to form West Virginia in 1863.

INDUSTRIALIZATION AND EXPANSION

With the Civil War over, Americans once again headed west. In 1862 Congress passed the Homestead Act. Under this law, the government would give up land it owned in the West. Men would receive 160 acres (968 sq km) of land after they lived on it or farmed it for five years. As a result, hundreds of thousands of poor Americans were able to acquire their first farms. Many settled in Kansas, Nebraska, and the Dakotas.

Early settlers on the Great Plains often built their homes out of brick-shaped chunks of grass and dirt called sod.

THE RAILROADS

Congress also expanded the nation's railroads. The first trains had appeared along the east coast in the 1830s. By 1860 rail lines reached as far west as St. Louis. To boost the growth of railroads, the government gave land to railroad companies. The companies then sold some of the land to pay for building their railroads. This practice had actually started east of the Mississippi before the Civil War. These land grants played a role in the settling of the Great Plains. This flat region sat between the Mississippi River and the Rocky Mountains.

The railroad companies and the settlers needed each other to survive. The railroads wanted customers to use their trains. The companies made money by transporting people and goods. Without the railroads, farmers would not be able to get their goods to market. The railroads also fed the growth of towns around railroad stations. The companies provided jobs for people who did not own farms.

Building the railroads

An engineer on a railroad project of the 1860s described the work: "At one time we were using at least 10,000 animals, and most of the time from 8,000 to 10,000 laborers.... To supply one mile of track with material and supplies required 40 [rail] cars... everything—rails, ties..., fuel for locomotives and trains, and supplies for men and animals...had to be transported from the Missouri River."

*In 1862 Congress made plans for a **transcontinental** railroad. Seven years later, workers in Promontory Point, Utah, celebrated finishing the railroad.*

THE INDUSTRIAL REVOLUTION

Growth of the railroads was part of the Industrial **Revolution**. Several decades before the Civil War, new industries began to appear across the United States. For the first time ever, large numbers of people left their homes to work in factories. Inventors created machines for making tools and products. Waterfalls and steam engines powered the new machines. Roads, canals, and railroads linked the people who made goods with a growing number of **consumers**.

Making **textiles** was the first important industrial activity in the United States. Later, railroads, coal, iron, and steel fueled the Industrial Revolution. Steam engines in factories and on trains needed coal to run. Iron **ore** was turned into iron, which was used for railroads and other metal products. After the Civil War, the ore was often used to make steel, which is stronger than iron. Iron and coal mines led to the growth of the steel industry and of cities such as Pittsburgh and Chicago.

Andrew Carnegie, a poor immigrant from Scotland, became a leader in the steel industry. When he sold his company in 1901, he became one of the richest men in the world.

CHANGES IN DAILY LIFE

In the early 1800s, the United States was a nation of farmers. The Industrial Revolution changed that. Young men and women left small farming towns for jobs in mills and factories. On farms, nature shaped the workday. Reduced sunlight in winter and bad weather limited when work was done. Inside factories, the work went on year-round through all kinds of weather. Gas, and later electricity, provided heat and light.

Electric industry

In the 1880s, several inventors found ways to produce large amounts of electricity. This energy was used to power trains and provide light inside factories and homes. Later, large electric motors also boosted industry. Factories no longer needed to haul in huge amounts of coal to power the steam engines that ran machines.

The textile mills of New England gave many women their first chance to work outside the home.

Thanks to improved tools, farmers doubled the amount of wheat they could grow.

INDUSTRIALIZATION ON THE FARM AND RANCH

The Industrial Revolution played a role in U.S. farming. New technology made it easier for farmers to produce more crops with less work. During the 1830s, Cyrus McCormick perfected a machine to cut wheat. Before this, farmers had to cut the wheat by hand. Other inventors designed new plows. Over time, the new farm machines were built quickly in large factories. The price for them fell, so more farmers could afford to buy them.

Industrialization also changed what Americans ate. For decades, American ate plenty of pork. After hogs were killed, the meat could be salted or smoked so it would not rot. As settlers moved west, they found large, grassy areas where cattle could graze. Using the railroads, ranchers could easily get their cattle to factories in the Midwest, where the animals were killed. Refrigerated trains, first used in the 1880s, meant beef could be sent long distances without rotting. Fresh beef could be sold and eaten anywhere in the country.

LONG-DISTANCE MESSAGES

Another important invention helped people communicate more quickly. The transcontinental telegraph line used electricity that traveled along metal wires. Telegraph operators stopped and started the flow of electricity to tap out messages using a special code. Before the telegraph, messages were carried by horse, trains, and boats. A letter might take days or weeks to cross the country. A telegraph was much faster. In the last two decades of the 1800s, telephones appeared. Still, the telegraph remained an important tool for communication.

Steam trains hauled live cattle from Colorado to cities such as Chicago for processing into meat products.

Making meat

Philip Armour focused on processing hogs in Chicago, which became the main meat-packing city in the United States. Armour hung animals on hooks attached to a chain, which then moved through his factory. Each worker cut just one part from the hog as it moved along. Armour's process lowered the cost of turning hogs into meat.

CONDITIONS IN THE FACTORIES

The Industrial Revolution provided millions of jobs, but conditions were harsh inside the mills and factories. Businesses made their workers, including children, work twelve hours a day, six days a week. Factories were hot and sometimes dangerous. Some workers lost fingers or limbs in machines. Steam engines sometimes exploded. In coal mines, workers breathed in harmful coal dust.

Improving these conditions cost money, so few businesses bothered. They felt that workers could always leave if they did not like their jobs. The owners knew that other Americans were willing to risk difficult conditions to get a paycheck.

Children under fourteen were allowed to work in most U.S. factories until the late 1930s.

In Baltimore, ten people were killed during the Great Strike violence.

UNIONS AND STRIKES

To improve pay and working conditions, workers began to form **unions** in the early part of the 1800s. The unions grew after the Civil War. In a union, workers had more power to get what they wanted. They could go on strike, meaning they could stop working to protest their company's actions. One worker alone risked getting fired by striking, but if all or most workers went on strike, the company was forced to shut down. The owners would then lose money.

Once workers could strike, companies would be forced to decide whether they were better off by improving salaries and working conditions. As more people joined the unions, their power became stronger.

Great Strike of 1877

The first nationwide strike in the U.S. took place in 1877, when the **economy** was weakened. Railroad companies had reduced pay for their workers. Railroad workers went on strike in West Virginia, and soon others joined them. The strike then spread to other industries with workers concerned about falling wages. The **federal** and state governments brought in troops to end the strikes. At least 50 people were killed before the Great Strike ended.

THE WESTERN FRONTIER

Railroads and industrialization made goods available all around the country. The **frontier**, however, had its own culture. Ideas and attitudes in the West were often shaped by the promise of greater personal freedom and wide-open space. The "rushes" westward for gold and other precious metals created new towns, called boomtowns. Denver, Colorado, and Portland, Oregon, joined San Francisco as major western cities.

Buffalo Bill Cody's "Wild West Show" featured fake gunfights, real Native Americans, and skilled shooters such as Annie Oakley.

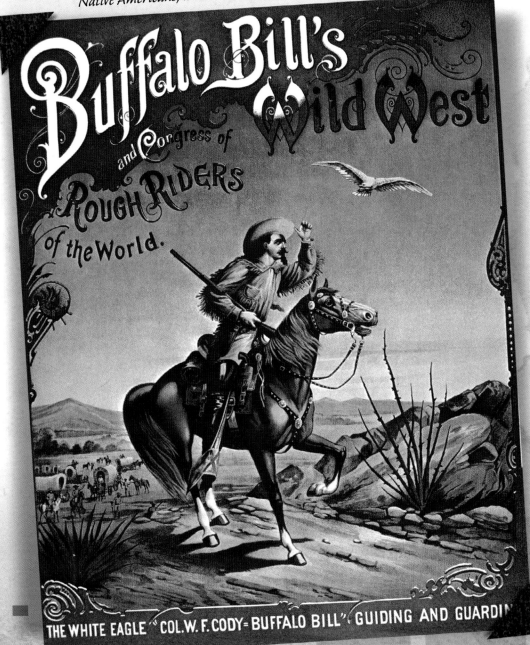

LAW AND ORDER

At times, new towns grew before people could set up strong governments. People needed to defend themselves and their homes from hostile Native Americans or other settlers. Guns were common. "Frontier justice" occurred when settlers acted as their own judges and jury.

Different groups in the West sometimes clashed as they struggled for money and power. Railroad companies, settlers, and ranchers all competed for land. At times, the groups fought to get their way. Each side used gunfighters who were skilled shooters.

Both law officers and crooks also killed people. Sheriff Wyatt Earp hoped to make money by bringing order to Tombstone, Arizona. He fought a famous gun battle at the OK Corral. One major criminal of the West was Jesse James. With his gang, James robbed banks and trains. He was killed by a gang member seeking the reward for James's capture or death.

Boomtowns such as Bodie, California, often became "ghost towns" when nearby mines closed.

THE NATIVE AMERICANS OF THE WEST

Many Americans saw the West as a vast, empty land. The region, however, was home to Native American **tribes**. Some had lived there for hundreds of years. Others had been forced from their lands in the East to live on **reservations** in Oklahoma.

The Comanche and the Lakota rode horses to hunt bison, which are also known as buffalo. Buffalo provided food, clothing, and tools that could be made from their bones.

Farther west, several different tribes lived in the Great Basin. This desert region is located between the Rocky Mountains and the Sierra Nevada peaks. The Shoshone, Ute, Washo, and other tribes hunted animals such as rabbits, snakes, and birds. North of the Great Basin, tribes ate salmon and other fish from rivers that flowed through the Rockies and the Cascade Mountains. The Nez Perce, Palouse, Klamath, and others of this region also gathered the plentiful berries that grew in the valleys.

Many western tribes lived in tipis, which are homes made of poles and animal hides (skins) that can quickly be set up and taken down.

U.S. settlers along the coast of the Pacific Ocean met some of the wealthiest tribes in North America. These included the Nootka, Chinook, and Nooksack. The ocean provided them with huge amounts of fish and sea mammals, such as seals and whales. The tribes also hunted in nearby forests.

The Spanish brought horses to Mexico, and they soon spread into the lands of Native Americans in the West.

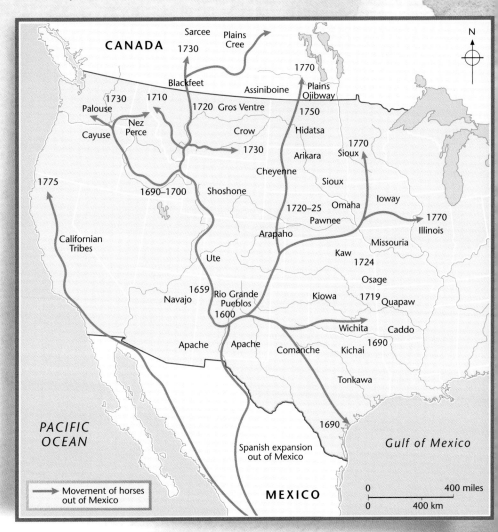

Native American religions

Like all Native Americans, the tribes living in the western part of the country had strong religious beliefs. Most Native Americans felt a deep connection to the natural world. They thought of the world as a living thing filled with spirits and forces that certain humans could contact. Religious figures called shamans were messengers between the spirits and humans. All tribes had religious ceremonies that featured dances. Each dance had its own goal. One might attract animals for hunting, while another might honor the dead.

NATIVE AMERICAN WARS

The United States' westward expansion led to conflicts with Native Americans. After the 1849 Gold Rush, U.S. troops fought Native Americans in California and elsewhere. In the 1860s, the fighting spread across the Southwest and Great Plains. The U.S. government wanted to force the Native Americans onto new reservations. Some tribes realized they could not defeat the Americans and went peacefully. Certain tribes, however, chose to fight.

During the 1880s, Geronimo led one band of Apache who rebelled against the U.S. government. He was captured in 1886 and spent the rest of his life as a prisoner of war.

MAJOR BATTLES

From 1874 to 1875, the Comanche and Kiowa attacked settlers in Texas. The U.S. Army fought back. Soldiers killed many of the tribes' horses and destroyed their homes. In 1876 Sitting Bull and Crazy Horse led the Sioux against U.S. forces at Little Bighorn, Montana. The Sioux won that battle, but still lost their lands. The final blow came in 1890, at Wounded Knee, South Dakota. U.S. troops killed more than 150 Sioux, including many women and children.

In the Southwest, the Apache fought U.S. troops for several years. Finally, however, they went to the reservations. Life was hard there for the Apache, since they often did not have enough food. Some of them left the reservations and began fighting again. The Apache wars lasted until the 1880s, when U.S. troops finally ended the rebellions.

Oklahoma land rush

Even Native American reservations were not safe from settlers. After forcing Native Americans to move to Oklahoma, the U.S. government forced the Creek and Seminole tribes to sell the land in 1889. Then, on April 22, Americans were allowed into the territory to claim the land. About 100,000 people rushed into Oklahoma that day. They took almost two million acres (8,094 sq km) of land in just a few hours. Oklahoma City had a population of 10,000 by the end of the day.

In 1867 General George Armstrong Custer and the men of the 7th Cavalry were massacred by Sioux and Cheyenne Indians at the Battle of Little Bighorn.

IMMIGRATION

The first European settlers came to North America searching for freedom and a better life. During the Industrial Revolution, millions of Europeans and hundreds of thousands of Asians arrived, seeking the same thing. The largest wave of immigration began toward the end of 1800s. Immigrants had many reasons to come to the United States. Some were attracted to the idea of owning their own farms. Others joined relatives who had already crossed the ocean and found success. At times, immigrants were pushed to leave by conditions in their homeland.

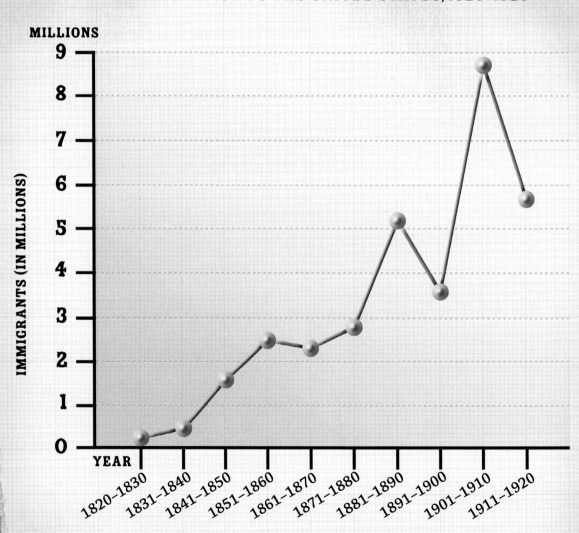

IMMIGRATION TO THE UNITED STATES, 1820–1920

MILLIONS

IMMIGRANTS (IN MILLIONS)

YEAR

1820–1830, 1831–1840, 1841–1850, 1851–1860, 1861–1870, 1871–1880, 1881–1890, 1891–1900, 1901–1910, 1911–1920

Not all of the millions of immigrants who came to the United States stayed there. Some returned to their homelands or moved on to other countries.

"NEW" IMMIGRANTS

Until the 1880s, most immigrants to the United States came from Great Britain and northern Europe. Ireland and Germany sent the most immigrants through the 1800s. After that, the immigrants came from a wider region, including Italy, Austria-Hungary, and Russia. Many French-speaking Canadians also moved to the United States.

In general, the so-called "new" immigrants settled where they could easily find jobs. That usually meant they moved to the growing industrial cities of the East and Midwest. New York City was home to large numbers of both old and new immigrants. Cities such as Cincinnati, Chicago, and Milwaukee had large German populations. Many Italians settled in small northeastern factory cities.

Ellis Island

The most famous place where immigrants arrived was Ellis Island, New York. The poorest immigrants were brought there for medical exams. People who were sick had to stay on the island until they were well or return to their homeland. Immigrants could also be sent back if they had ever been to prison in their homeland. Immigrants who met all the requirements were allowed to enter New York City. For them, Ellis Island was the "island of hope." But for the unlucky ones who had to return home, Ellis Island was called "the island of tears."

During the Industrial Revolution, immigrants did much of the hard work in U.S. factories.

GETTING SETTLED

As they settled in the United States, immigrants faced many hard tasks. Most did not speak English. They usually arrived without much money, but they had to find somewhere to live. Then, they had to find a job.

Immigrants often chose to live in neighborhoods with other members of their ethnic group. These were people who came from the same country and spoke the same language. Immigrants from the same ethnic group also came together to share their old culture. They kept many of their old ways while becoming **Americanized**. They often went to churches where their native language was spoken. The immigrants also ate the same foods they did at home.

COUNTRIES OF ORIGIN FOR FOREIGN-BORN RESIDENTS IN VARIOUS CITIES, 1910

New York

Russia	484,000
Italy	341,000
Germany	278,000

Chicago

Germany	182,000
Austria-Hungary	161,000
Russia	122,000

Lawrence, Massachusetts (a mill town near Boston)

Canada	8,000
Italy	7,000
England	7,000

This chart shows the homelands of the largest immigrant groups in several U.S. cities in 1910.

LIFE IN THE CITY

Since many immigrants were poor, they would rent rooms in boarding houses. Large families would live in tiny apartments called tenements. These buildings were often located in poor sections of a city, called slums. Crime was common, and the tenements often did not have heat or clean water.

To make money, all members of a household usually worked. Some families did piece work. This means they made items of clothing or other goods and were paid for each piece they made. As families earned money, they moved out of the slums and into larger housing. Some immigrants used their savings to start businesses.

Jane Addams

In 1889 Jane Addams of Chicago opened Hull House. Addams was part of the Progressive Movement. Its members tried to help workers and immigrants during a time of rapid industrialization. At Hull House, the poor received food and could take English lessons. Addams also provided daycare for the children of working mothers. Hull House was the first settlement house. In a settlement house, immigrants received the tools they needed to survive in a new land.

The rooms in tenements had few windows, so they were usually hot and dark.

IMMIGRANTS OF THE WEST AND SOUTH

Some new immigrants headed to the Great Plains to farm. These newcomers included a large number of Russians who had once lived in Germany. In the South, New Orleans was a major port for shipping goods. Many Italians settled there to buy and sell fruits and vegetables. Immigrants also moved to fishing communities in the South and West. These cities included San Francisco and Galveston, Texas. Some new immigrants found work when gold and other metals were discovered. New and old immigrants built the railroads that crisscrossed the country.

Between 1877 and 1887, about two million people, like these Swedish immigrants, settled on the Great Plains.

THE APPEAL OF CALIFORNIA

Decades after the Gold Rush of 1849, California still attracted a large number of immigrants. The state offered rich land for farmers and a long coast for fishermen. Italian and French immigrants who settled there created the first major wine industry in the United States. German and Swiss immigrants in California often turned to dairy farming. Many Chinese worked in mines and on the railroads.

One of the new immigrant groups to arrive in California was the Japanese. Only a few thousand came to the United States before 1890. From that year until 1910, hundreds of thousands arrived. Most of the Japanese went to California, where they often worked for U.S. farmers. After saving money, they bought their own farmland. The Japanese farmers usually grew fruits and vegetables.

The Potato King

George Shima was one of California's most famous Japanese immigrants. He came to the U.S. in 1889 with money and settled in the San Joaquin Valley. There, he drained swampland to use it for farming. Shima was known for growing potatoes, which led to his nickname—the Potato King. By 1913 Shima employed 500 people.

Many Asian immigrants' first stop in the U.S. was Angel Island, in San Francisco. The immigrants went through the same exams that Europeans faced at New York's Ellis Island.

HARSH ATTITUDES

Most of the old immigrants were Protestants. Many of the new European immigrants were Roman Catholic or Jewish. The Asians practiced non-Christian religions, such as Buddhism, that were unfamiliar to most Americans. Many Protestants considered these faiths **inferior** to their own. Some Americans feared the new immigrants would not be able to understand the country's democratic society and become good citizens. These people were called **nativists**. They ignored the fact that they were once immigrants, too. The nativists' **prejudice** made them lash out at the new immigrants.

Some Americans blamed immigrants for strikes or violent acts, such as this 1886 riot in Chicago's Haymarket Square.

ATTACKING THE IMMIGRANTS

Nativists were not new in the United States. Back in the 1840s, the Irish had faced this attitude. After the Civil War, the Chinese were the next target of prejudice. At times, Americans and European immigrants clashed with the Chinese. In 1885 white miners in Wyoming killed 28 Chinese miners. No one was punished for the murders.

By that time, the nativists had already won a legal battle. In 1882 Congress passed a law that ended Chinese immigration to the United States. Around that time, nativists were also demanding that immigrants take literacy tests. The tests would show if the immigrants could read and write. Over the next few decades, nativists would keep trying to screen out certain immigrants.

These immigrants did not meet the requirements of the new immigration laws and were sent back to their homelands.

1882	**1885**	**1891**	**1907**	**1917**
The Chinese Exclusion Act is introduced. An immigration act charges a 50-cent tax on each immigrant.	Contract Labor Law limits bringing in workers hired outside the country.	An immigration act prohibits the entry of certain people, such as convicts and the mentally ill.	"Gentlemen's Agreement" between Japan and the United States sharply limits Japanese immigration.	An immigration act adds a literacy test and expanded limits on all immigration from Asia.

OVERSEAS EXPANSION

After the 1860s, some Americans began looking beyond North America for further expansion. The major European nations were building empires. This meant they took control of foreign lands so they could acquire their natural resources. The United States did not want to be left behind in this race for empires. In addition, as international trade grew, the United States would need distant ports where ships could take on fuel.

The first major new territory added was Alaska. The United States paid $7.2 million for this former Russian **colony**. Some Americans thought the price was too steep and the land was worthless. But in the end, the purchase proved valuable. During the 1880s and 1890s, gold was discovered there.

This map shows U.S. territories in and near the Pacific Ocean, with the year they were acquired.

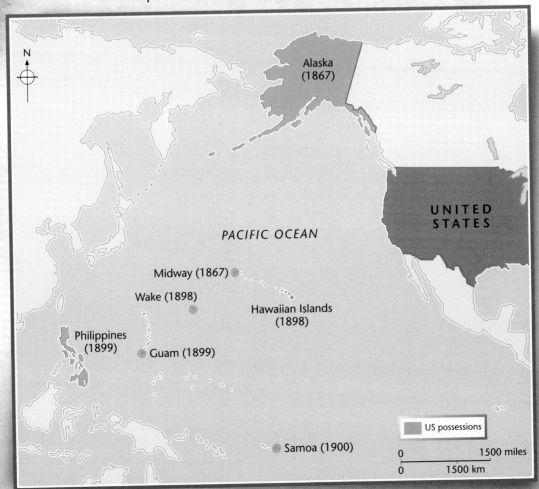

N

Alaska (1867)

UNITED STATES

PACIFIC OCEAN

Midway (1867)

Wake (1898)

Hawaiian Islands (1898)

Philippines (1899)

Guam (1899)

US possessions

Samoa (1900)

| 0 | 1500 miles |
| 0 | 1500 km |

PACIFIC ISLANDS

Through the mid-1800s, U.S. ships often stopped in Hawaii. At the time, Hawaii was an independent kingdom. U.S. businesses raised sugarcane there. In 1893 U.S. citizens living there forced the queen out. Five years later, the United States **annexed** Hawaii.

Also in 1898, the United States and Spain went to war. The main issue was Cuba, a Spanish colony. The mysterious destruction of a U.S. warship in Cuban waters led to war. U.S. forces quickly took control of Cuba and the Philippines, a Spanish colony in Asia. When the war ended, the United States kept the Philippines and also received Puerto Rico and Guam from Spain. Cuba became independent, but was under tight U.S. control.

The *Maine* in Cuba

In January 1898, President William McKinley sent the battleship *Maine* to Cuba. He wanted to protect U.S. citizens there. On February 15, 1898, an explosion sank the battleship. Many angry Americans assumed that Spanish forces had blown up the *Maine*. Newspapers demanded a war, and public feelings against Spain shaped McKinley's decision to fight. Historians now believe that an accident on the *Maine* led to the explosion.

*The first U.S. citizens living in Hawaii were **missionaries** such as Richard Lyman, who built this house in 1839.*

A DEBATE OVER EMPIRE

Acquiring former Spanish colonies thrilled some U.S. leaders. The Philippines were considered to be especially valuable. The colony produced sugar, an important crop. The Philippines would also serve as a base for trade with China. European nations were already doing business in China. The United States hoped to compete with them.

Some Americans saw **imperialism** as a new stage of manifest destiny. Senator Albert Beveridge said, "We are a conquering race. We must... occupy new markets, and if necessary, new lands." Other Americans, however, opposed imperialism. The United States had started out as series of colonies. Americans had disliked being ruled by a foreign nation. The country should not now have colonies of its own.

Some anti-imperialists believed the United States would have to use force to govern distant lands. They disliked violence and thought imperialism denied the rights of the colonists. Other anti-imperialists wanted the country to focus on problems at home. The United States should not spend money building an overseas empire. The anti-imperialists included industrialist Andrew Carnegie and the author Mark Twain.

COL. THEO. ROOSEVELT.

Theodore Roosevelt, who supported imperialism, led soldiers called the Rough Riders in Cuba during the Spanish-American War.

Emilio Aguinaldo was supported by the U.S. when he led Filipino rebels against Spain. When the U.S. decided not to grant independence to the Philippines in 1899, Aguinaldo started the rebellion against the U.S.

Troubles in the Philippines

Some of the anti-imperialists' concerns were sparked by fighting in the Philippines. The Filipinos had wanted their independence from Spain. Now, many of them refused to live under U.S. rule. Starting in 1899, Filipino rebels fought some 125,000 U.S. troops sent to the islands. Both sides committed horrible acts of violence. About 4,000 U.S. troops died fighting the Filipinos, many of them from disease. The main fighting ended in 1902, with the U.S. government firmly in control.

CHANGES IN A NEW CENTURY

In the years after the Spanish-American War, the United States became an industrial giant. Immigration peaked in the first decade of the 1900s. During that time, more than eight million people arrived in the country. The United States became the world's largest producer of steel and iron, and the automobile was a growing source of transportation. The first cars with gas-powered engines had appeared in Europe in the 1880s. Americans, however, soon created the world's largest auto industry. Henry Ford led the way. He made cheap cars that many people could afford.

Henry Ford perfected a system called mass production to make his cars. Workers built just one section of a car over and over, using identical parts.

WORLD WAR I

In 1914 a member of Austria's ruling family was killed. Germany, Austria's **ally**, encouraged Austria to seek revenge. Because of various **treaties** among the European nations, many countries were soon at war. The United States, however, chose not to get involved. President Woodrow Wilson knew that each side had supporters in the United States. He did not want to seem to favor one group of Americans over another.

The United States traded with both sides, but mostly with Great Britain. The British were battling Germany and its allies. In 1917 Germany increased its attacks on U.S. ships traveling to Europe. Wilson then decided to enter the war. Several million U.S. troops went to Europe. In 1918 they helped the British and their allies win the war.

The oil industry

The modern oil industry began in Pennsylvania in the 1850s. Companies dug wells into the earth to pump oil to the surface. Gasoline was one product made from oil. The development of gas-powered cars led to a search for more oil. In the early 1900s, oil was found in Texas and other western states. That discovery led more Americans to these areas to look for jobs.

When the United States entered World War I, President Woodrow Wilson said, "The world must be made safe for democracy."

41

THE RED SCARE

At the end of World War I, Americans had many concerns. The flu killed many people and the economy was slowing. Workers across the country were going on strike. Immigration remained a major concern for some Americans. Nativists wanted new limits on who could enter the United States.

Some Americans began to fear that immigrants would use violence to spread their political beliefs. In 1919 U.S. officials began to arrest suspected **communists**. Many of them were immigrants. Some were forced to leave the country, even though they had not committed a crime. The color red was associated with communism, so this period in U.S. history is often called the Red Scare.

For most of the 1920s, the U.S. economy was strong, and the decade was called the Roaring Twenties or the Jazz Age.

CLOSING THE DOOR

In 1921 Congress decided to set quotas, or limits, on immigration. The Quota Act was only supposed to last one year, but Congress made it permanent in 1924. The final law was based on population figures from the 1890 **census**. This was before the huge numbers of eastern and southern Europeans entered the United States.

The Quota Act of 1924 ended the great immigration boom of the industrial era. A few years later, another boom came to a painful end. In 1929 the **stock** market crashed. The United States' faith in its great wealth and ability to grow received a shock. As the country entered the Great Depression, several dark years lay ahead.

Sacco and Vanzetti

Nicola Sacco and Bartolomeo Vanzetti were Italian immigrants and communists. In 1920 they were arrested for murder. The men insisted they were innocent. Because of their beliefs and ethnic background, they could not get a fair trial. Their case became national news as they tried to win their freedom. Finally, in 1927, Sacco and Vanzetti were executed. They were punished for a crime they most likely did not commit.

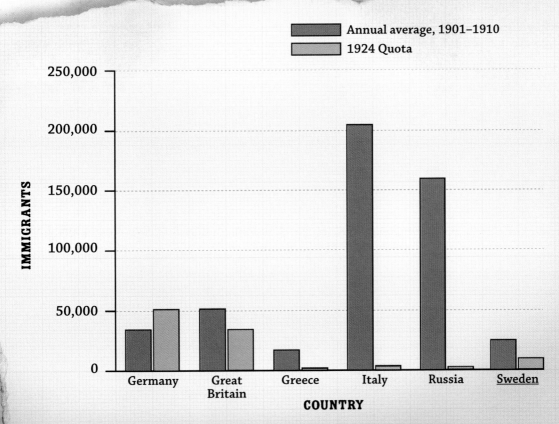

This chart shows the effects of the 1924 quota on immigration from some countries.

IMMIGRATION TO THE UNITED STATES

This chart shows the country of origin of the major immigrant groups for the period from 1841 to 1920 and notable facts about their experiences.

GERMANY

Peak years: 1841–1890: 4.3 million arrivals. Included Jews, as well as Poles living in land controlled by Germany.

Settlement: Widespread, with large populations in New York and midwestern cities and towns

Particular reasons for leaving: Political troubles at home; had skills in demand in United States

GREAT BRITAIN

Peak years: 1841–1890: 2.65 million arrivals. Included residents of England, Scotland, and Wales.

Settlement: Widespread

Particular reasons for leaving: Had skills in demand in United States

IRELAND

Peak years: 1841–1900: 3.6 million arrivals

Settlement: Widespread, but particularly in northeastern cities

Particular reasons for leaving: Famine and lack of jobs in Ireland; harsh policies of Great Britain, which ruled Ireland at the time

SCANDINAVIA (NORWAY, SWEDEN, AND DENMARK)

Peak years: 1861–1910: 1.9 million arrivals

Settlement: Primarily in the Midwest

Particular reasons for leaving: Shortages of farmland at home

CHINA

Peak years: 1851–1890: 290,000 arrivals

Settlement: California and other western states

Particular reasons for leaving: Drawn by California Gold Rush and lack of jobs in China

ITALY

Peak years: 1881–1920: 4.1 million arrivals

Settlement: Primarily northeastern cities, plus California and Louisiana

Particular reasons for leaving: Drought, disease, and high taxes in homeland

AUSTRIA-HUNGARY (EMPIRE OF CENTRAL EUROPE THAT NO LONGER EXISTS)

Peak years: 1881–1920: 4 million (included Poles, Czechs, Slovaks, Hungarians, and Jews) arrivals

Settlement: Primarily cities of the Northeast and Midwest

Particular reasons for leaving: Desire for jobs, escape prejudice

RUSSIA

Peak years: 1881–1920: 3.2 million (included Poles, Germans, and Jews) arrivals

Settlement: Primarily cities of the Northeast and Midwest

Particular reasons for leaving: Desire for jobs, escape prejudice

JAPAN

Peak years: 1891–1920: 239,000 arrivals

Settlement: California and other western states

Particular reasons for leaving: Desire for jobs

TIMELINE

1846 The United States and Mexico go to war.

1848 Gold is discovered in California; the United States acquires California and New Mexico from Mexico.

1850 Compromise of 1850 allows residents of the New Mexico and Utah territories to choose if they want slavery.

1854 Kansas-Nebraska Act allows slavery north of the 36° 30' line of latitude.

1861 The Civil War begins.

1862 The Homestead Act makes it easier for settlers to own land in the Great Plains and the West.

1865 The Civil War ends and slavery is outlawed across the United States.

1867 The United States buys Alaska from Russia.

1869 The first transcontinental railroad is completed.

1876 Sioux Indians defeat U.S. troops in South Dakota.

1877 The "Great Strike" begins in West Virginia and spreads across the country.

1882 Congress passes the first immigration law to limit the arrival of one specific ethnic group: the Chinese.

1889 In Oklahoma, U.S. settlers are allowed to claim land previously owned by Native Americans, sparking the Oklahoma Land Rush; Jane Addams opens Hull House to help immigrants adjust to life in Chicago.

1898 The United States annexes Hawaii; the country defeats Spain in the Spanish-American War.

1899 The United States takes control of Puerto Rico, the Philippines, and Guam from Spain.

1917 The United States enters World War I.

1921 Congress passes the first quota law, limiting immigration from Europe.

1924 Congress passes the Quota Act of 1924.

1929 The stock market crashes, helping to cause the Great Depression.

GLOSSARY

abolitionist person who wanted to end slavery everywhere in the United States

ally person or country that helps another achieve a common goal, such as defeating an enemy

Amendment new section added to the U.S. Constitution

Americanize to learn the culture and beliefs shared by most U.S. citizens

annex take control of land not previously part of the country

border dividing line between one country or region and another

casualty person killed or wounded during a war

census count of the number of people living in a particular area

civilian person who is not in the military

colony land not connected to a nation, yet owned and controlled by it

communist person who believes that the government, not private citizens, should own factories and land

compromise agreement that settles an argument, with each side giving up something it wants

Congress part of the U.S. government that makes the country's laws

constitution system of laws in a country that state the rights of the people and the powers of the government

consumer person who buys goods and services

democracy form of government in which citizens make political decisions as a group or elect others to make those decisions for them

economy total of goods and services produced in a country or region

federal central government

frontier largely unsettled border areas of a region or colony

fugitive person who runs away from slave owners or law officials

immigrant person who arrives in a new country after leaving his or her homeland

imperialism political and economic system that stresses gaining overseas territories, to benefit the country that gains them

independence freedom from another person's or country's control

inferior not as good as

latitude imaginary lines used to measure distances north or south of the Equator

missionary someone who is sent by a church or religious group to teach that group's faith or do good works, especially in a foreign country

moral relating to what is right and wrong

nativist person who dislikes immigrants

natural resource mineral, plant, or other item from the earth that is used to make products

ore mineral that contains a valuable substance that can be removed and turned into products

party group of people who share the same political views and goals

political relating to the government and how it runs

prejudice dislike for a group because of their race, religion, or other trait

reservation land set aside for Native Americans by the U.S. government

revolution sudden and huge change in ideas or actions

secede to break away from a larger group or government and become independent

settler person who moved from one place into a new region

slavery system of buying, selling, and keeping people who were forced to work for their owners for no pay

stock part ownership in a company

territory area of land under the control of a government; part of the United States that has its own government but is not yet a state

textile cloth used to make clothing

transcontinental going from one end of a continent to the other

treaty written agreement between two or more countries

tribe group of people who share the same ancestors, customs, and laws

union group of workers who come together to seek better pay and work conditions

FURTHER READING

BOOKS

Brezina, Corona. *The Industrial Revolution in America: A Primary Source History of America's Transformation into an Industrial Society*. New York: Rosen, 2004.

Isaacs, Sally Senzell. *The Gold Rush*. Chicago: Heinemann Library, 2004.

Josephson, Judith Pinkerton. *Growing Up in Pioneer America, 1800–1890*. Minneapolis: Lerner, 2002.

Kupferberg, Audrey E. *The Spanish-American War*. San Diego: Blackbirch, 2005.

Marker, Sherry. *Plains Indians Wars*. New York: Facts on File, 2003.

McPherson, James M. *Fields of Fury: The American Civil War*. New York: Atheneum Books for Young Readers, 2002.

Sandler, Martin W. *Island of Hope: The Story of Ellis Island and the Journey to America*. New York: Scholastic, 2004.

Stefoff, Rebecca. *Growth in America: 1865–1914*. New York: Benchmark, 2003.

Worth, Richard. *Westward Expansion and Manifest Destiny in American History*. Berkeley Heights, N.J.: Enslow, 2001.

INTERNET

Gold Rush
http://www.calgoldrush.com

Perspective on the American West
http://www.pbs.org/weta/thewest/

Museum of Westward Expansion
http://www.nps.gov/jeff/mus-tour.htm

The Iron Road
http://www.pbs.org/wgbh/amex/iron/

Ellis Island
http://www.ellisisland.org/genealogy/ellis_island.asp

The Age of Imperialism
http://www.smplanet.com/imperialism/toc.html

Jane Addams Hull-House Museum
http://wall.aa.uic.edu:62730/artifact/HullHouse.asp

Disclaimer
All the Internet addresses (URLs) given in this book were valid at the time of going to press. However, due to the dynamic nature of the Internet, some addresses may have changed, or sites may have changed or ceased to exist since publication. While the author and Publishers regret any inconvenience this may cause readers, no responsibility for any such changes can be accepted by either the author or the Publishers.

INDEX